This book belongs to:

Happy Retirement!

Retiring gives you a fresh chance to think, journal and plan your future. This lined journal is a great way to keep track of notes, ideas, travel plans, bucket lists and other retirement musings. Plan your novel, take notes on a course – or just use it for your shopping lists!